MEMORIES OF GLASGOW

Part of the
MEMORIES *series*

Contents

First published in Great Britain by True North Books Limited. England HX3 6SN. 01422 244555.
www.truenorthbooks.com. Copyright © True North Books Limited, 2012

ISBN 978 - 1906649821. Text, design and origination by True North Books
Part of the 'Memories' compact series and based on the original Memories of Glasgow publication.

Memories are made of this

Memories. We all have them; some good, some bad, but our memories of the city we grew up in are usually tucked away in a very special place in our minds. The best are usually connected with our childhood and youth, when we longed to be grown up and paid no attention to adults who told us to enjoy being young, as these were the best years of our lives. We look back now and realise that they were right. So many memories - perhaps of the war and rationing, perhaps of parades, celebrations and Royal visits. And so many changes; one-way traffic systems and pedestrianisation. New trends in shopping led that to the very first self serve stores being opened.

Through the bad times and the good, however, Glasgow not only survived but prospered. Fine old buildings continue to dominate the city centre, and besides the many monuments and sites of historical interest which have been preserved and restored. None of the city's experiences have gone to waste; instead they have combined to make Glasgow such an interesting place, full of character. We have only to look at the city as it is today, with its finest buildings now cleaned and restored to their full glory, and the traditional tourist attractions now complemented by up-to-the-minute facilities, to see what progress has been realised and what achievements have been made. So sit back and enjoy the ride, as we take you on a pictorial meander through the streets of our great city.

Off on its way to Kelvinside, passing the cake and grocery store, the tram is taking shoppers and office workers to their homes in the northwest end of Glasgow. It will go out past the Victorian splendour of Kelvingrove Park and the less than splendid tenements on the way. There were also some grand houses around there, which have since become offices.

The streets of change

Looking at the George V Bridge in 1929, it must have been a quiet part of the day. Normally, there would have been a fairly heavy throng of people and traffic shuffling along. However, there may be another reason. It is the era of the depression. The bridge in view has some similarities with its neighbour, Jamaica (Glasgow) Bridge, which is to the right of the railway bridge you can see. The parapet of the George V Bridge could almost be a carbon copy. However, there are only three arches. In fact, these are not true arches, being disguised spans of concrete box girders. Reinforced with concrete, the roadway is 80 ft wide and runs 412 ft from Commerce Street to Oswald Street. It was opened in 1928. In the previous century, this stretch of the Clyde used to see small steamers travel to such far-flung destinations as Stornoway and London, Sligo and Southampton.

Tramcars, loaded with travellers on their way to who knows what or where, clank across Jamaica Bridge. It was a time of change, one of many in the 20th century. The Great War had been fought and the free world was rebuilding, at a cost. Andrew Bonar Law, a partner in one of the city's largest iron manufacturing and exporting firms, had briefly been Prime Minister. But, by the following year, 1924, Britain would see its first Labour government. The majority of the tram-riders would have been happy with that. Towering above the cars, carts and pedestrians, those on the upper decks had a fine view up and down the river. There are now

seven traffic, four pedestrian, two railway and one motorway bridge to contend with. Towards the end of the 18th century there was but one medieval bridge for all cross-river transport. It had been built in 1450. The one in the picture was the third on this site and is also known as Glasgow Bridge. On wintry days, Glaswegians would have been grateful for a warming cup of Bovril, advertised in the lower left of the picture. A steaming cup of the tangy beef extract warmed the cockles of many a chilled heart and their fingers and throats, too!

This elevated view shows a number of the varied features that mark out Glasgow as a special city. The marvellous architecture in the foreground is repeated throughout its many elegant streets. There are beautifully preserved Victorian buildings, none more splendid than the City Chambers. In and around there are unique examples of the renowned designer, Charles Rennie Mackintosh. The famous Glasgow School of Art is another of his masterpieces.

The Lambhill tram on Renfield Street had just reached the crossroads with St Vincent Street, where it was to cross the path of another of its fellow vehicles carrying passengers ready to shop until they dropped. In 1958 the tills rang merrily as we stocked up with Tide or Omo washing powder. The man on the right looks like a news vendor carrying copies of the Evening Times back to his newspaper stand.

Cowlairs Co-operative Society dominated the retail outlets at Springburn Cross. As well as the shops carrying its own name, most of the other businesses operated from premises owned by the Co-op. From their rents Cowlairs Co-op got its own form of 'divi' which helped the payouts made to its customer members. By 1900 the population here had grown to 30,000. This was a vibrant working class district. Most were in employment connected with the railway. The majority lived in the tenements that had become part and parcel of Glasgow life. Rents were often paid annually. This presented budgeting problems for the less sophisticated worker. Saving for future commitments at the Clydesdale and North of Scotland bank at the corner of Cowlairs Road did not come easily.

Away to the right, Springburn Rd, Flemington Rd and Atlas Rd sweep away towards the rail stations at Springburn and Barnhill. Opposite, Keppochill Rd runs away towards the recreation ground at Cowlairs Park. In the 1950s local residents happily went about their business and went off to work at the workshops and repair yards at Cowlairs and St Rollox. Others were involved in the locomotive building taking place at the Hydepark and Atlas works. The Beeching report of 1967 changed all that. The community was suddenly thrown into an era of massive unemployment. No longer could you go to McNee's for some bath salts for mum's birthday present or to the dentist's on the first floor at Keppochill Rd corner.

Much criticised by purists for scarring the city, though it is hard to see how we can move without it, the M8 motorway has ripped through what was the St George's Cross of 1938. All sorts of shops could be found around here in those last days of uneasy peace before the second world war. The House of Fraser, which once dominated Glasgow's shopping scene with a large number of outlets, owned the Wood and Selby store. Other competing shops and stores included Duncan's and Woolworth's, both of which were on the right hand side, looking east. St George's Cross was a very busy junction, feeding traffic from Springburn, Maryhill and Possilpark into the city centre. The traffic policeman at the crossroads is in for an active day.

MEMORIES OF GLASGOW

The grandly carved buildings on Renfield Street, leading north from the city centre, stand majestically above the line of trams on their way to Mosspark and Pollokshields. These areas are now cut by the M77, one of the motorway links criss-crossing the city borders. Back in 1936, public transport carried the people of Glasgow to and from the city to carry out their business or to do their shopping. It is only from such an elevated view that the magnificence of the architecture can be appreciated.

MEMORIES OF GLASGOW

At the beginning of the 20th century Glasgow was the 'second city of the Empire'. As one of the finest and richest cities in Europe its museums, galleries and public buildings were the envy of all. The retail outlets and businesses along Renfield Street mirrored the success of the other important streets in the area. Busy bowler-hatted men, on their way to the office, used to vie with the barrow boys selling secondhand books. The Council would later ban these booksellers as they were thought to lower the tone of the district. But, as the purse strings were tightened, establishments like RG Lawrie found life becoming tougher. Flags were flying bravely above the doorway as if to show a pride in still being there.

The long avenue of Sauchiehall Street stretches east from Charing Cross. The Coronation trams, a permanent feature on Glasgow's streets in 1938, were a new line, having replaced the older and less reliable Standards. Making their way towards the Grand Hotel, from where this photograph was taken.

Situated on the corner of Newton Street, which is now flanked by the motorway, Skinner's tea rooms opened his business here in 1835. It would continue as a going concern until tastes changed and the demand for the relaxed atmosphere of the tea room was no longer needed. It closed in 1961. Opposite, McColl's shop had a clock face set into the building. The face later vanished, but became a working clock once more in 1970.

As this tram passes along Trongate and away from the steeple, further along on the left, towards Argyle Street, note the clothiers. In grandma's time there was a host of such shops around here. From late Victorian times, with the coming of the sewing machine, the making of clothes became a factory based industry because of the speed of these machines and the volume that could be handled. The factories sold direct to shops, as well as exporting their goods. D & H Cohen made all the skirts and trousers sold by the huge chain of Marks and Spencer. They also specialised in uniforms for schoolchildren.

It's a quieter day at Charing Cross. Sauchiehall Street reaches down towards its junction with Renfield Street in the far distance. In 1949, the ration coupon had been with us since the start of the decade. It wouldn't finally become a thing of the past until 1955. Transport changes were coming subtly to the city's streets by now. The tram, although it would still be around for another ten or a dozen years, was losing its influence as the main form of public transport. Charing Cross marked the end of the entertainment and shopping focus which was Sauchiehall Street.

It was a good pull up the hill coming away from Balgrayhill. These pictures are the only real way to hold on to memories of old Springburn. Nearby was the Springburn North UF church at the corner with Elmvale Street. United in 1967 with Springburn Hill, the vacant church was vandalised and then demolished. Above Maguire's pub were the Argyll Halls that held dances and various other social functions. The pub became Healy's Terminus bar and the Halls a singing lounge. Ex Celtic footballer, Chris Shelvane, later owned it. These days and those that went before can only be recalled properly by artefacts and photographs. As fewer of those who lived through the time remain with the passage of time, community museums, like the one at Atlas Square become more important. Only by preserving these can future generations gain an accurate picture of the past.

A sunny late summer day in the 1950s, with the lengthening shadows falling across Springburn Rd. Beyond the Kirkcaldy Linoleum Market, the low building on the right is the railway station. The Cowlairs Co-operative Society on the left was just one of 110 outlets across the city. These were the streets that were the playground for the comedy actress, Molly Weir. Her fame spread from local reps and concert parties down to the theatres and studios of London. Springburn was proud to see one of its daughters return via the TV screen in a number of character parts in plays and sitcoms. She wouldn't have recognised it these days. The Royal cinema has gone. Formerly the Ideal, it had started life as Springburn Electric Theatre. Gone, too, is the fire station, which was near the corner with Keppochill Rd. In 1986 that part was converted into flats and modern housing for elderly residents.

Pictured on Argyle Street, not far from the Tron on Trongate, this old chap has seen better days. Who knows what difficulties have brought him to spend his life in a state of hopeless despair. He might have been a hero of the second world war of 20 years before, when he fought to enable the young schoolboy coming towards him to be free. The demise of the heavy industry of the shipyards and the railways saw thousands of jobs disappear. Men who had brought home bulging pay packets were, along with the ships they built, on the scrapheap. Being unable to provide for the family any more drove so many over the edge. He is left to tramp the pavements looking for a few bob for a meal and a place to rest his head for the night. Folk singer Ralph McTell used to ask, 'Have you seen the old man who walks the streets of London?' Maybe not, but we've seen more than enough on the streets of Glasgow.

In sickness and in health

The beginning of Glasgow's campaign to eradicate the scourge of tuberculosis from the city was marked by an official launch in George Square. It was March 9th, 1957, and the gathering of 10,000 people on that Saturday evening was entertained by the band of the Highland Light Infantry and the Glasgow Police Pipe Band as they waited for the speeches and the cutting of a ribbon outside the X-Ray Centre by two youngsters which would signal the start of Europe's biggest ever health improvement campaign. Specially-positioned searchlights painted patterns in the sky and a fireworks display would later enthrall the crowds as 37 athletes carried Olympic-style torches with the 'X-ray' message to every Ward in the city. Among the runners taking part were famous names such Dunky Wright and marathon men Ian Binnie and Graham Everett. Every day an average of 17 new cases were diagnosed on average in the city. A target of 250,000 X-ray examinations was set for the campaign.

A floodlit George Square was the venue for the launch of the Glasgow campaign against tuberculosis in 1957. The campaign would last five weeks and break all records as the largest of its type ever to be seen in Europe. TB had long been a problem in Glasgow where the highest incidence of the disease existed of anywhere in Europe. Over 6000 new cases had been reported in 1956, slightly down on the previous year, but still a huge burden on local medical resources and the local community. It was estimated that the disease cost the city over £1 million each year - on top of the inestimable cost in terms of human misery.

Sunday March 10th, the day after the launch of the campaign, saw an impressive parade of mobile X-ray units in the city centre. The Lord Provost 'took the salute' as the heavy trucks, laden with state of the art equipment, snaked their way around the narrow streets, much to the delight of the cheering crowds. In all, 30 mobile X-ray units had been draughted in for the campaign; 24 from England, and six from other areas of Scotland. Each vehicle weighed 10 tons and was 26ft in length. The trucks were manned by one doctor, two nurses, four clerks, two typists and the driver.

Every available means of publicity was employed in order to promote awareness of the TB campaign. This illuminated tram carried the message around the city, proclaiming "Everybody over 14 years X-Ray now" and reassuring people of the ease, confidentiality and need not to undress for the X-ray. The message was put across at football clubs, cinemas and other places of entertainment. A light aircraft from Nottingham was enlisted to fly over the city with a recorded message urging people to have the test blaring out from powerful loudspeakers. Crawling across the skies at a height of 1500ft the speakers proclaimed 'Go to the nearest X-ray centre and get your friends too go as well!'

Queues at the main X-ray centres in George Square were extensive - even when the weather was less than pleasant. The X-ray itself was said to take only a fraction of a second once the 'patient' had managed to secure his or her place in the booth. Official 'hostesses' would look after any accompanying children while mum or dad had their X-ray. There were two queues - one for men and the other for women at each centre. Up to 300 people per hour passed through the main units in the centre of Glasgow, and additional city centre screening facilities were provided at two large department stores. The first day of the campaign saw over 20,000 people tested - a world record in itself. By the third day over 80,000 people had had their test, and confidence was high that the 250,000 target for the campaign would soon be smashed.

Above: Scotland's own Jimmy Logan was one of the first to sign up as a volunteer helper in the TB campaign. He was not alone, for the massive undertaking relied upon the help of no less than 11,000 volunteers who had freely given their time to play a part in the fight against TB. An obvious use of Jimmy's talents was to promote the awareness of the campaign. He was soon asked to record a song with that aim, called "An X-Ray For Me". The song was sung to the tune of "A Gordon For Me" with words written by Archie Gentles, a member of staff at Glasgow Corporation Health and Welfare Department.

Bottom Right: Massive amounts of publicity and awareness for the campaign. One tool in their armoury was a promotion designed to give everyone having an X-ray the chance to win exciting prizes. These ranged from a family saloon car (an Austin A35, complete with insurance and concrete garage!) to a washing machine, television set, holiday in the Highlands and a bedroom suite. all the prizes were sponsored by local firms. In this picture Max Bygraves (who was appearing at the Glasgow Empire) can be seen presenting the prize of a washing machine to David Henderson (second from the right), a 35 year old polisher from Drumchapel. Max Bygraves had his own X-ray after the presentation was completed.

Right: Glasgow's anti-TB campaign would only be a success if it persuaded all age groups (over 14 years) to take part. From the start it was recognised that younger people may be difficult to influence, and at least two songs were written and performed to help get the message across. This picture shows Bill Lambert and his band performing the song "X-Ray Rock". The song was written by a local health worker, Doctor Bill Thomson, with music by his friend Alex Bunting, a chartered surveyor in the city. After a recording of the tune by Bill Lambert and his band was approved by the Medical Officer of Health the order was given to produce 'dozens' of records to be played at dance halls, cinemas and football grounds.

Other methods employed to encourage the young to come forward for their X-rays included the staging of a film premier, The Rainmaker at the Gaumont. Greta Reid, vocalist, can be seen here with Bill Lambert's band - Bill himself is pictured with his treasured saxophone.

Such was the attraction of the prize draw in the TB campaign, that several reports of people having two or more X-rays were reported, these people being referred to as 'twicers' - their actions intended to give them an extra chance of winning one of the exciting prizes on offer. The famous American pop singer Johnnie Ray in the 1950s and he is seen here presenting a fridge to 14 year-old Sandra Stevenson of Maryhill. At £70 this would have been a luxurious item in 1957 for sure. Reports from the time describe how Sandra was called from her maths class to the headmasters' office to be told of her win. Her main concern was her meeting with her pop idol. "I am awfully thrilled to be meeting Johnnie Ray - I wish I knew what to say to him!" she said. The main prize of a car, complete with concrete garage, was awarded at the end of the campaign after a televised draw was made by none other than Petula Clarke. The draw was made on a teatime TV news programme and, remarkably, the police were sent, lights flashing, to bring the winner, Miss Tomlinson, into the studio before the end of the show. Even more remarkably, and against all the odds, Miss Tomlinson was a TB sufferer herself.

Below: This large scoreboard-style indicator was positioned at George Square and designed to track the progress of the various Glasgow districts towards the overall target in the TB campaign. Glasgow had been described as the TB blackspot of Europe, and the 33 day long campaign was intended to be the turning point in the battle against the disease. 50,000 posters had been displayed throughout the district to publicise the campaign, and the pages of every local and regional newspaper carried reports of how the campaign was being organised and managed. Metal badges were given to people after their X-ray had been carried out, and the whole city buzzed with excitement and curiosity as the major undertaking got underway.

Above: Last minute queues at the end of the TB campaign resulted in most of the stations remaining open well after the scheduled closing time of 10.00 a.m. The George Square facility was open until midnight, the last X-ray being performed on Police Constable Robert Maxwell, aged 41, who was presented with a £5 voucher by Mr Bailie Mains, Convenor of the Health and Welfare Committee. Astonishingly, a total of 43,700 people had an X-ray on the final day of the campaign - making a total of 712,860 for the five week period. In all, a total of around 7,000 people had been found to be suffering from the disease, and the more serious cases were soon sent off to the allocated hospital beds for treatment.

On the move

Large shops and stores which occupied corner positions on Glasgow's streets often liked to claim them as their own. On Charing Cross you could find Massey's Corner. Here, on Trongate, as it leads out to London Road, was Lawson's Corner. In case you weren't sure of Lawson's importance, the message was repeated as 'Lawson's of Glasgow Cross'. Further towards the bridge were Benson's and McEwan's. The area around Glasgow Cross quickly became a rough and lawless place to be. The housing was just as bad and residents were amongst the unhealthiest in Glasgow, so insanitary were the living conditions.

Times change, but, then again, perhaps they don't. Small single decker buses carrying people in and out of the city had their day. All of a sudden, they are back with us. Private companies used to provide services in the 1920s. At the end of the century, with deregulation in force, they were back on the streets once more. Nippier and smaller than the double decker, they cause less congestion and keep traffic moving more smoothly. The bus in the photograph looks as smart and gleaming as a new Dinky toy. The driver is ready to set off on the western run to Paisley. The route followed a similar line taken by the M8 as it sweeps out beyond the home of the Thomas Coats Observatory. In 1937 the government sponsored the building of the large industrial estate that was home to some 150 factories.

MEMORIES OF GLASGOW

By the late 1950s the city centre was becoming a nightmare. It's probably Saturday and Lewis's and the other department stores are no dought doing a good trade as the pavements are choc a block with shoppers. Traffic on the road seems to have come to a standstill. The incident being attended to by the fire service hasn't helped, nor has the lorry in front. However, just look at the row of trams. Their inflexibility of movement, stuck to the tramlines as they were, slowed everything to a snail's pace. The increase in the number of private cars on the road had also contributed towards the mayhem. Whilst Glasgow had a comparatively low level of car ownership, the traffic flow needed restructuring. Trams were last to run in 1962. Trolley buses had been introduced in 1949, but these were tied to the overhead cable route and followed the trams out in 1967. The rail and bus services were improved. In 1960 the suburban electrified rail network was opened and one man-operated buses came a few years later. By the end of the 1990s, 39 per cent of all journeys are made on public transport, with four times as many people being carried on buses rather than by rail.

Coming towards us is the No 37 to Castlemilk. Its journey from here on Springburn Rd takes it to the south of the city, out beyond Rutherglen. This area, around Vulcan Street and Cowlairs Rd, was known as Springburn Cross. It is now totally unrecognisable, as the demolition and regeneration of the later part of the 20th century has torn down most of what you see. The new expressway and motorway, added to the shopping centre and modern housing has destroyed the character of Springburn. In the 50s, this was a busy little spot, a community in its own right. Going back to the end of the 18th century, it was a village that was home to weavers, farm labourers and men who worked in the quarries.

MEMORIES OF GLASGOW

Everybody outside Glasgow knows about the city's main street: Sauchiehall Street. This, though, is just not true. To the native, Buchanan Street was the one that held pride of place as a shopper's paradise. If you want any further proof, just look at what's happening in 1948 as you look south from the eastern end of Sauchiehall Street. This is a time of austerity, remember. Despite rationing the street is teeming with people and cars. Buchanan Street always has been that little bit special. today cars are banned completely in the pedestrian area, safe in the knowledge that no wildly driven Morris Cowley is going to make you jump back on to the pavement. Before the motor-car crowded the road, the absence of the tram helped Buchanan Street retain an air of superiority as a centre of quality and value. Formed in the 18th century, it first became important for its luxury department stores. Here, shops such as H Samuel's jeweller's, Burton's tailor's, Lizar's optician's and the Clydesdale Bank illustrate the variety offered to the shopper of the time.

Charing Cross Mansions is one of the few to have survived from this 1929 view of an area that was one of those extensively remodelled in the 1970s. When people from out of the city speak of tenements they often think of slum dwellings, but the beauty of this curved block gives the lie to that impression. It was originally built in 1891 for the warehousemen Robert Simpson & Sons and is a distinctive landmark, with its ornate clock and carved figures. On the left, the Grand Hotel had seen many famous and titled people pass through its doors.

Above: Great Western Road has always been a busy and dangerous highway. The overtaking car is good evidence of the slogan once taught to children, 'Stop, look and listen'. McColl's fruiterer at the Botanic Gardens also specialised in wedding bouquets. Fresh fruit and flowers for sale. Many a young beau would stop here to buy a posy or a rose for his loved one. The popular Kenneth McKellar singing 'My love is like a red, red rose' might inspire later generations. The park and gardens behind led down to the River Kelvin and, with the exotic Victorian Kibble Palace in the background, were a romantic spot to be charmed by the attentions of the lad on your arm. In the meantime, the Glassford Street bus waits for passengers from the station that was here from 1910 until it burned down in 1970.

Right: The Scottish Daily Mail has the news that counts, or so it claimed around 1960. It's around the time when prime minister Harold Macmillan had told us that we had never had it so good. People were packing the streets to try to prove him right, as shop cash registers started ringing again. The prosperity of the rest of Britain didn't reach Scotland to the same degree, but it was better than those first postwar years when austerity and rationing made us wonder who had really won the war. Great matters of the economy were of little interest to these two boys. As long as they had their pocket money, they were content. A sherbet dip and a read of Roy of the Rovers in the Tiger lay ahead for them as they fingered the pennies in their fingers.

The new world and the old meet at Central Station. The trams, around in one form or another since the 1870s, pass one of the swish models of the day. The young man at the wheel of this 1960 Sunbeam was proud of his convertible. The 'Alpine' was one that had a real sporty image. Anything that linked with Americans was also an enviable fashion item. Their music, hairstyles, clothing and movies were all the rage, or should one say 'hip'. today, they would be 'wicked'. Del Shannon singing 'Runaway', the Tony Curtis cut and this lad was in his element. Over to the right, Burton's tailors could be relied upon to provide the Saturday night suit. Casual dressing for a date or a dance was still on the horizon. The smart man was also a smoker. The Capstan medium cigarette was a popular brand. The driver was going under the place where people often used to congregate after church - the 'Hielanman's Umbrella' which carried the old Caledonian Railway.

High days and holidays

The main entrance to Springburn Park was via the wide promenade of Broomfield Rd. It led to the bandstand and Winter Gardens. In the early years of the 1900s the middle class made their homes in this part of Springburn. Walking around there you would be rubbing shoulders with doctors, ministers, teachers and prosperous publicans. This was of no consequence to the children sailing their little home-made boats on the waters, keenly hanging on to the strings which they held in their hands. In the background a brass band would be playing to old men and women fast asleep in their deckchairs. In 1892, AB MacDonald, the City Engineer, laid out the 58 acres that the Corporation had bought for £25,000. A year before his death in 1894, the respected industrialist James Reid donated the bandstand. A memorial to him was unveiled in 1903.

Every city, in 1936, had its Locarno. The civil war in Spain and the rearming in Germany were a world away when, on a Saturday night, you could put on your glad rags and go up to Sauchiehall Street at Charing Cross and dance to your heart's content, or until the last bus or tram was due. If you were really lucky, there might be a nice, young chap to walk you home. If you were very lucky, a fish and chip supper on the way would be even better. Dancing to live bands is something the young of today know little of. Their grandparents danced holding each other "cheek to cheek", as did Fred Astaire and Ginger Rogers in the 1935 movie Top Hat. The more energetic had their moments, too. The jitterbug, the forerunner of the jive, had come from America and shocked the more staid dancer by its wild freewheeling. Still, there was always the last waltz to look forward to. The Benny Daniels Orchestra continued to play here for many years after the war. The Locarno later became a casino.

Bird's eye view

Looking north across the Clyde and the city centre, in the foreground of this aerial view from about 1950, the sweep of the railway across the bridge and into Central Station stands out clearly. Also clearly prominent are the lines of commercial buildings and tenements that mark out Buchanan Street, Renfield Street, Blythswood Street, Newton Street and others. Glasgow has had a roller coaster of a population over the last two centuries, rising and falling quite dramatically. In 1800 there were but 77,000 people living here. By the time of World War I this had rocketed to six figures. The massive increase meant that there was both a housing shortage and tremendous overcrowding. Disease in these conditions was widespread. Glasgow was known as the tenement city. By the time the population peaked at over 1,100,000 at the start of World War II, most lived in one or two roomed tenement houses. These buildings were occupied from the cellars to the attics. In the 1940s and 1950s the City Council struggled to provide decent housing. In 1951 half of Glasgow's tenements had no inside bathroom and TB was rife. Major slum clearance schemes produced mixed results. Some regeneration merely produced modern high rise slums in the 70s.

MEMORIES OF GLASGOW

The aerial view of the city shows the crowded and congested nature of Glasgow in the early postwar years. Probably dating from 1949, towards the left of this photograph Central Station can clearly be seen. The scene across the city, leading north from the river, has altered in the 60 years that have passed since this view. The first recognised centre of shopping in Glasgow developed in and around Glasgow Cross. In the 19th century, the commercial focus shifted west to the Sauchiehall Street/Argyle Street/Buchanan Street area, at the centre of this picture. The roads to be seen coming out of the city were lined with shops, above which large tenements loomed. The clearance of the inner city slums meant the loss of some traditional shopping areas. Some of the older ones, such as Springburn, Maryhill and Govan have been redeveloped. Glasgow is still the largest city in Scotland, boasting a population of over 600,000. However, this is only just over half of the peak figure of over 1,100,000 in 1939. The Bruce Plan of 1945 reduced housing densities and proposed new radial transport routes and industrial estates.

MEMORIES OF GLASGOW

The writer, Daniel Defoe, spoke of Glasgow as a large well built city. He admired the grandeur of the stone buildings that made it one of the best and cleanest places in Great Britain. He was writing around 1700. At this time most Glaswegians lived around High Street and Saltmarket. The old town grew round the Cathedral, spreading gradually down to the Clyde. Defoe would have been referring to the large mansions that were developed on Buchanan Street, Queen Street and Virginia Street by the wealthy merchant class. Life had changed dramatically in the period leading up to the time captured in his photograph. The Clyde had become as central to Glasgow's prosperity as it is to the photo. Steam driven weaving machinery had helped the cotton and textile industry grow in importance and the ships of the Clyde gave easy access to overseas ports for both imports and exports. In one year alone, 105 million yards of American raw cotton were spun into thread. Some of it was taken down river and across the seas to India. The chemical industry grew around the textile business, supplying bleaches, dyes and stains for cloth.

Events & occasions

Central Station in the early 1900s is wall to wall with people. The railway lines were built at a low level, so the steam and grime from the locomotives had further to go to disperse. Many a tickle in the throat and many a soiled collar and cuff were the result of being in Central Station too long. It's not forever, though. today is Fair Saturday. Mid July and for two weeks we can forget our troubles. Trainloads of holidaymakers will descend on the Clyde coast to escape from the oppression of the city. Out will come the buckets and spades at Largs and Fairlie. Others would take the paddle steamers to Dunoon and Rothesay. More intrepid souls would venture further afield to the foreign shores of Blackpool and even the Isle of Man.

Although rationing is still around, the sense of deprivation has started to ease as 1952 draws to a close. There should be enough for a good spread at home when the relatives come to join us for Christmas lunch or a drink and a mince pie on Boxing Day. The members of the Salvage Corps, their wives and sweethearts, pose under the streamers and decorations ready to swap yarns, enjoy a dance and a dram or two at the recreation hall. Wind up the gramophone and put on a Jimmy Shand record and have a good old-fashioned party. The younger ones who want to dance to the latest pop sensation, Johnny Ray or whatever he's called, can wait. The Gay Gordons and an Eightsome Reel are the ones for a proper Christmas party.

MEMORIES OF GLASGOW

Processions and parades have long been part of our national heritage. Some of them, particularly those proclaiming certain religious allegiances, have not always been accepted universally. However, there are no such problems with this one in Springburn Park. Hundreds gathered by the bandstand to watch the Temperance King and Queen lead the way across the lawns. The movement against alcohol abuse had long gathered force in Glasgow and many other large cities. Seeing the housekeeping blown in the bars had blighted too many lives. Fuelled by booze, men often became violent both in the home and on the street. The Saturday night punch-up was an all too common sight. The temperance movement tried to encourage family events as one way of distracting people from alcohol. The well scrubbed king looks a tad embarrassed to be walking alongside his pretty but girly queen. Its a good job they didn't have to hold hands. For her it would remain a proud moment in her upbringing. The other little girls holding the train might be excused a little jealousy, but perhaps one of them would rise to the dizzy heights of royalty next year.

On the home front

In the 1920s, the Glasgow Salvage Corps headquarters were to be found on Albion Street. Here, members of the corps sit proudly aboard two of their appliances. The Glasgow Corps was the last of three to be formed in the UK. The other two were in London and Liverpool. A number of fires in the city in the 1860s led the Insurance Committee to set up the Corps at its first station on Nicholas Street in 1873. There were eight full-time members with just one horse drawn trap. These men worked as an organisation independently of the fire brigade. Their job was to reduce the amount of damage and loss in a fire, so reducing hardship and helping business resume as soon as possible. Obviously, this saved the insurance companies money. The main problem was water damage, not the fire itself. The first superintendent was Edwin Goodchild, who held the position until his death in 1887. Around this time, the Corps moved to the station on Albion Street, from where it operated until 1972.

'They shall grow not old, as we that are left grow old. Age shall not weary them, nor the years condemn.' The words of Laurence Binyon that are spoken at every Remembrance Day service up and down the land each year. Although meant to commemorate the fallen in the two world wars, the service acts as a focal point of remembrance for all who have made the ultimate sacrifice in the defence of others. Included in our thoughts on the second Sunday in each November are those brave police and fire officers who perished helping others, as well as members of the armed forces. Here, in the 1960s, William Noddings, Ronald Bevan and Peter Gilligan prepare to pay their tribute by laying the Salvage Corps wreath at the War Memorial. On the day of this photograph, there will have been many veterans from the second world war paying homage to old comrades.

MEMORIES OF GLASGOW

The power of fire and the total disregard for anything in its way was brought home to the people of Glasgow that horrid day on 28 March 1960. About 20,000 barrels of whisky and other spirits were thought to have been held in a six storey bonded warehouse in Cheapside. Fire had been reported in a neighbouring building and Granston Street Fire Station crew attended, accompanied by the Salvage Corps. Within the hour, the fire had taken hold and spread quickly. Without warning, a huge explosion ripped out the sides of the warehouse. Fourteen fire service personnel and five salvagemen were killed. The city was stunned. Princess Margaret visited, to pay the respects of the Royal Family. Services were held at Glasgow Cathedral and St Andrew's Cathedral. Fire crews from all over Britain sent a contingent to share the city's loss. The Lord Provost launched a disaster appeal that raised £180,000. Two firemen were awarded the George Medal and three others the British Empire Medal. The solemn men in the photograph are attending the dedication of the plaque on Albion Street to the Salvage Corps men who perished that sad day. 'The name of Cheapside will forever bear a hallowed place in the history of the city of Glasgow, recording the supreme sacrifice of so many fine and courageous firefighters.'

IN MEMORY OF
THE OFFICER & MEN
OF GLASGOW SALVAGE CORPS
WHO LOST THEIR LIVES
IN THE DISASTROUS FIRE
CHEAPSIDE STREET GLASGOW
28TH MARCH 1960
SUPT E C MURRAY
L/S/M J A McLELLAN
S/M W OLIVER
S/M J F MUNGALL
S/M G C McMILLAN

Bridgeton Cross is out along the London Road at the east end of the city. Parkhead, the home of Celtic Park where Glasgow Celtic plays its soccer matches is only a short distance away. The ornate tram shelter was both functional and an architectural delight. These structures were dotted along the tram routes and this one has been preserved as a living part of Bridgeton. The police box for emergency use was a common feature on our streets, even in the 1960s. British police boxes were usually blue, except in Glasgow, where they were red until the late 1960's. In addition to a telephone, they contained equipment such as an incident book and first aid kit. They are now best remembered as the home of the Tardis, the space and time ship of the TV character Dr Who. Played originally by William Hartnell, we all remember the exploits of the eccentric Doctor and his battles with those most frightening of enemies, the Daleks. Sadly, the box has long gone from Bridgeton.

The WVS appeal and distribution centre had organised salvage collections for the RAF. Aluminium pots and pans, kettles, saucepans, jelly moulds and colanders were gathered from Glasgow homes and around. From the first such collection over 1,000 tons of metal salvage was realised. It was heartening to think we had contributed to that Spitfire protecting our skies, though it was difficult to believe it was some form of flying frying pan! In this photograph, the sorting mainly concentrates on the toys and clothes that have been gathered. Some lucky toddler will soon be whizzing around on that trike. 'What can you do?' asked ARP posters at the beginning of the war. More women than men responded by volunteering their services as Air Raid Wardens and many were then recruited by the WVS. Then, they certainly found plenty to occupy them, valuably and usefully, too. Responding to the needs of others was a true war effort.

The war effort wasn't all about scavenging metal for new warplanes. There were any number of appeals for clothing and toys for displaced and unfortunate families. Here WVS members are surrounded with items collected or sent in to help those who were in need. The WVS became an official clothing distribution centre for Glasgow Corporation. The Post Office would provide the transport and delivery of the results of the appeal and the women would then leap into action. The dollies would bring joy to the hearts of little girls whose homes had been flattened by the 1941 Clydeside blitz and those of later Luftwaffe raids.

Purposefully striding out on their way to a church service, these ladies of the Women's Voluntary Service celebrate the fifth anniversary of its formation. Sensible shoes and a sturdy uniform typify the resolve of these women. Theirs was a practical role, born of the necessity of wartime. This wasn't a group of well meaning middle class women holding coffee mornings and chatting about the war effort. They did something about it. It was the army that Hitler forgot. By July 1943 they had much of which to be proud. Air Raid Precaution had slowly been developed during the 1930s and the WVS was founded in 1938 as a support to the ARP.

On the hotline to Churchill? Whoever she was talking to, the WVS member on the right wouldn't have been chatting idly. Pencil in hand, she was seeking important information to help others passing through Central Station in May 1944. The soldiers leaning through the hatches came to rely on the help these women could give them in finding their way across the country. As well as the British, many soldiers from overseas, Poles, Free French, Americans and Canadians, passed through Central Station on their way to new billets or off on a short leave. The WVS assumed the role of guides or information officers. These Glasgow guides were to meet every troop train, day or night, throughout the war. Many a Tommy would pretend to need a personal escort from a younger Service member to find his way across the city, but she had heard all the lines before. A sweet smile and a knowing look was the only response he was likely to get. Still, you couldn't blame him for trying.

In 1940, the mobile emergency feeding canteen appeared on Glasgow streets. Men had become used to seeing women driving ambulances, lorries and vans during the Great War, so there was little sexist objection to the woman behind the wheel of the canteen. Certainly there wasn't from these chaps. The Women's Voluntary Service gave support when there were food supply problems, something that was to become more important as the war continued. After a fire or a bombing, the canteen would arrive with a warm meal and hot drink to give refreshment to the emergency services and feed those who had been driven from their homes. The WVS was formed in 1938 and Lady Reading became its first chairman. Recognising that war was coming, the WVS organised first aid and gas defence classes for civilians.

By the time of this 1940 view of the WVS mobile canteen, Queen Elizabeth (now the Queen Mother) had become the Service's president, thus giving royal approval of the work being done. This became official in 1966 when it became the WRVS, the Women's Royal Voluntary Service. The canteen had been presented by the Scottish Iron and Steel Scrap Association. As well as giving out food to the deprived, after the first large bombing raids on our cities in World War II the canteens developed through and after the hostilities as support vehicles in times of major disasters. There were to be food convoys for the disaster areas, 18 Queen's Messenger Convoys being developed - a sort of food flying squad.

Down at the docks

Hundreds of high-pitched voices, chattering, laughing and squealing with delight; it's a threat to the eardrums. The paddle steamer Eagle III is leaving Broomielaw in 1929 on an outing. The occasion is a special one as it's a trip for the children from the Quarrier's Home. To make it even more special, this was the centenary year of the birth of the founder of the homes, William Quarrier. He was born into a poor family, but became wealthy as a self-made businessman with a string of shoe shops. Touched by the plight of a poor, young match-seller he saw in the East End of Glasgow, he opened his first home for such wretches in Renfrew Lane in 1871. Sixteen miles from the city is the village that was built to get away from the dormitories and workhouse style of other orphanages. It is, possibly, from this village that the excited hordes have come on this day to go 'doon the watter' and have a day to remember.

MEMORIES OF GLASGOW

The Sailors' Home, from where this photo was taken, was a hostel at 150 Broomielaw. Bought at a cost of £12,000 in 1856, it was extended in 1906. The decline of Glasgow as a major port after World War II led to its demolition in 1971. Seen from the old Sailors' Home, with its round tower and time ball, the George V Bridge was built at a height of 18 ft above the high water level. This let small coasting vessels pass under it on their way to and from Broomielaw. In the 19th and early 20th centuries, this section of the river would have been a highway of shipping sailing between the lines of the quays. Transatlantic steamers of the Anchor, Allan and Donaldson lines provided regular services

taking emigrants to the United States and Canada. Cargo steamers brought in food for the growing population and sailed out again, loaded with pig iron, coal and machinery. John Masefield's poem, 'Cargoes', could well be adapted to refer to these. 'Dirty British coaster with a salt-caked smokestack'. Looking across the Broomielaw sheds and beyond the bridge, the city centre businesses carry on their trade, knowing that access to the markets of the world can be gained from the Clyde quayside a short distance away. To the right are the fringes of the much criticised district of the Gorbals. The bridge names of George V, Victoria and Albert provide a link with the past.

The change in Glasgow's prosperity has never been more marked than in the changing fortunes of the shipyards. Govan docks. In 1966, the Geddes Report said that there were insufficient grounds, whether it be for social reasons or to bolster the balance of payments, to continue to build a lot of ships. It concluded that it might be better to let the industry decline. This sounded the death knell for yards on the Clyde. It was all a far cry from the halcyon days of years ago. In 1864, London & Glasgow Shipbuilding and Engineering opened at Govan. Harland & Wolff took over in the early 1900s and built the world's largest ship, the Olympic. The company also erected the nearby tenements for its workers. Between 1860 and the start of World War I over one third of all British shipping was built on Clydeside. From the building of the first steam powered ships in the early 19th century to the steel built ones at the end of the century, the Clyde led the world. Yards here, at Partick and Scotstoun built them all, from yachts to cargo vessels, from warships to submarines.

At the shops

The car turning at the crossroads between Argyle Street and Jamaica Street clearly dates this photograph. It's a troubled era in America. You can almost see Eliot Ness and the Untouchables jumping on to the running board and chasing Al Capone down the street, machine guns blazing. No such uproar in the Glasgow of 1930. Shopping is the order of the day, not prohibition. God help the politician who tried to introduce that piece of legislation here! Argyle Street was once a two mile stretch from Trongate to the Kelvin. The M8 motorway has now bisected it and the street disappears for a while around Anderston, before reappearing further west. Back in the 1820s, the architect, John Baird, designed the 480 ft dog-leg of the Argyle Arcade. Influenced by London's Burlington Arcade, Glasgow's answer was a number of top establishments, which later mainly concentrated upon the jewellery trade. Back in the early days such outlets as Galetti's sold mirrors and optical glasses, but later diversified into model yachts, steam engines and locomotives around the turn of the century. Here, the scene is of Simpson's Corner, with the name of Robert Simpson proudly displayed on the Jamaica Street awnings. Round the corner, on Argyle Street, is the place of many an ill spent youth, the billiard hall. The goods at One Price, lower right, turn the heads of the man pushing the barrow. What did he fancy for 16s 9d? These days, the eastern end of the street is dominated by the St Enoch Centre, sometimes known as the Great Greenhouse because of the huge amount of glass in the structure.

Don't be fooled by the name on the building by the traffic light. 'Edinburgh Warehouse 30 Princes Street' is tricking you into believing for a moment that you've suddenly slipped eastwards to that city on the Firth of Forth. You're still in Glasgow, just across the way from Central Station. At the corner of Gordon Street and Renfield Street, Saxone's was claiming the corner for itself. Crocodile leather shoes and winkle pickers were in vogue. Dad wasn't convinced. He 'couldna get his tootsies in those things' was how he put it. The shoe shops had their origins in the leather industries of Victorian times.

Roll up, roll up! The great sale is now on. Discounts for everyone. Don't you tire of those TV adverts for the great discount stores which offer furniture sales etc that must end on Sunday? The only trouble is, the very same advert appears next week and the week after and the week after .... But it's not just a phenomenon of the 1990s. Forty years ago (and more) they were at it, albeit in a more restrained fashion. The man in the sandwich board was a cheap way to get the message around town. You couldn't miss him as he, rather miserably, ambled up and down the road, hoping the rain would keep off. Tomorrow might see him with a different set of boards. 'The end is nigh' or 'Repent ye all sinners' were other messages to be carried along the cobblestones. Who took any notice? But they carried on doing so, anyway. Unfortunately, most people seem to be ignoring the message of the Argyle Warehouse.

It's a fine day in Glasgow city centre. In St Enoch Square, looking north towards Buchanan Street, shoppers merrily move from the shoe shop at Trueform, past H Samuel's jeweller's, at the MacDonald Argyle Street frontage, to Montague Burton's store. The Tardis wouldn't survive much longer. It belonged to a bygone age, as it was now 1976. The flared trousers of the younger generation crossing the square contrast with the oldfashioned garb of the women in front of the police box. St Enoch Square goes back to the 1770s. There used to be a church at its heart, but that disappeared in 1925. By the time pictured, the dramatic listed building of St Enoch Station and its Hotel were soon to be swept away. The station had terminus of the old LMS line.

The trams and cars that travelled along the roadway in 1950 have long gone as all traffic has been removed from this now pedestrianised part of Glasgow. The Savoy Shopping Centre has since appeared on the left, though it has retained the frontage that was once the Cumming and Smith Building, with its grand columns rising up through three storeys to the beautifully designed figures above, crafted by WB Rhind. Sauchiehall Street is second only to Buchanan Street in its importance as a shopping area, but it was formerly a fashionable place to live when early 19th century merchants made their homes here.

With very special thanks and appreciation for their help and contribution:

Newcastle Chronicle and Journal

The Ward Philipson Group

Beamish Museum